God's Little Instruction Book for Kids

LITTLE BITS OF WISDOM FOR LITTLE PEOPLE

Honor Books, Inc. • P.O. Box 55388 • Tulsa, OK 74155

All Scripture quotations are taken from the *International Children's Bible, New Century Version*. Copyright © 1986, 1988 by Word Publishing, Dallas, TX 75039. Used by permission.

God's Little Instruction Book for Kids
ISBN 1-56292-345-5
Copyright © 1994 by Honor Books, Inc.
P.O. Box 55388
Tulsa, Oklahoma 74155

INTRODUCTION

God has lots of good ideas on how we are to live,
How we are to love, and how we are to give.

This little book will help you to grow and know God's ways,
If you follow what it says and live it day by day.

A NOTE TO PARENTS

God's Little Instruction Book for Kids is based upon the #1 bestseller *God's Little Instruction Book*. It has been written and designed for children, and includes quotes, rhymes and bits of wisdom kids will cherish. Also included with each quote is a Scripture verse which unlocks the true meaning of the principle behind the quote.

Read the quote and Scripture to your child, and ask them if they understand its meaning. If they don't, explain it to them—show them how God's Word is relevant in today's society. Don't be embarrassed if you, yourself, like reading *God's Little Instruction Book for Kids*; it was meant to be treasured and enjoyed by anyone who is young at heart.

What you sow
is
what you grow.

A person harvests only what he plants.

GALATIANS 6:7

Whistle in the dark.
Whistle in the day.
Whistle as you work.
Whistle as you pray.

No matter where you are
or the situation there.
Whistle as an act of faith.
Whistle as a prayer!

Always be happy. Never stop praying.

1 Thessalonians 5:16–17

Beauty shines through
In the good that you do.

Your beauty should come from within you—the beauty
of a gentle and quiet spirit. This beauty will never disappear,
and it is worth very much to God.

1 PETER 3:4

"I'm sorry, forgive me,"
Are hard words to say.
But when said from the heart
They bring great joy your way.

But if we confess our sins, he will forgive our sins.
We can trust God. . . . He will make us clean from all
the wrongs we have done.

1 JOHN 1:9

Those who are tardy
May miss the party.

The "right time" is now.

2 CORINTHIANS 6:2

Obey now,
<u>Play</u> later.
Disobey now,
<u>Pay</u> later.

If they obey and serve him [God],
the rest of their lives will be successful.
And the rest of their years will be happy. But if they do not
listen, they will die . . . without knowing better.

JOB 36:11–12

Two wrongs never make a right.

Be sure that no one pays back wrong for wrong.

1 THESSALONIANS 5:15

Love the Lord your God.
Love him with all your heart,
all your soul, all your strength,
and all your mind.
Also, you must love your neighbor
as you love yourself.

LUKE 10:27

A VERSE TO MEMORIZE

Make the one who's been left out your special friend.

Do for other people what you want them to do for you.

LUKE 6:31

Hugs multiply
when you give them away.

Give, and you will receive.
You will be given much. . . . The way you give to others
is the way God will give to you.

LUKE 6:38

A smile
Never goes out of style.

Be full of joy in the Lord always.

PHILIPPIANS 4:4

A stitch, in time, saves nine.

If a person is lazy and doesn't repair the roof,
it will begin to fall. If he refuses to fix it,
the house will leak.

ECCLESIASTES 10:18

When you get a lemon, Make lemonade!

You meant to hurt me.
But God turned your evil into good.

GENESIS 50:20

Love has a way of not
looking at others' sins.

1 PETER 4:8

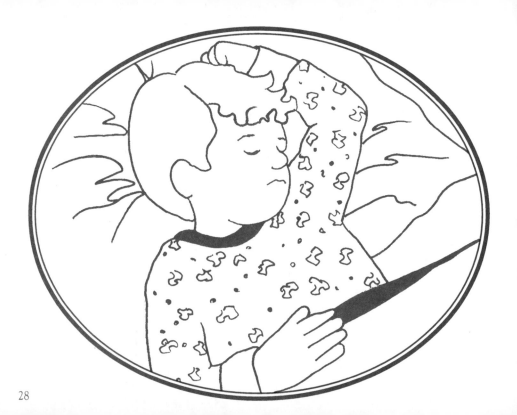

Good thoughts
create
sweet dreams.

Think about the things that are good and worthy of praise.

PHILIPPIANS 4:8

Take care to share.

Do not forget to do good to others.
And share with them what you have.

HEBREWS 13:16

Love listens.

We can come to God with no doubts.
This means that when we ask God for things
(and those things agree with what God wants for us),
then God cares about what we say.

1 JOHN 5:14

Sin is what the serpent says is "in."

You must not do wrong just because everyone else is doing it.

EXODUS 23:2

Sometimes we are
asked to wait.
But this we know—
God's never late!

The Lord is good to those who put their hope in him.
He is good to those who look to him for help.
It is good to wait quietly for the Lord to save.

LAMENTATIONS 3:25-26

God can do everything!

LUKE 1:37

Find someone with
a hole in their heart
and fill it with
God's love.

God has poured out his love to fill our hearts.

ROMANS 5:5

Whatever you say,
Whatever you do,
Bounces off others
And comes back to you.

Do for other people the same things
you want them to do for you.

MATTHEW 7:12

Soft words
are pillows
for hurts.

A gentle answer will calm a person's anger.

PROVERBS 15:1

For God loved the world so much
that he gave his only Son.
God gave his Son so
that whoever believes
in him may not be lost,
but have eternal life.

JOHN 3:16

THE "**BE**" ATTITUDES

Rely on
God's supply.

Those people who know they have great spiritual needs
are happy. The kingdom of heaven belongs to them.

MATTHEW 5:3

THE "**BE**" ATTITUDES

Problems
are
opportunities
in disguise.

Those who are sad now are happy.
God will comfort them.

MATTHEW 5:4

THE "**BE**" ATTITUDES

Little ones
to Him belong,
They are weak
but He is strong.

Those who are humble are happy.
The earth will belong to them.

MATTHEW 5:5

THE "**BE**" ATTITUDES

To delight
in the right,
Makes you big
in God's sight.

Those who want to do right more than
anything else are happy. God will fully satisfy them.

MATTHEW 5:6

THE "BE" ATTITUDES

To others be kind,
And you will find
kindness coming
back to you.

Those who give mercy to others are happy.
Mercy will be given to them.

MATTHEW 5:7

THE "BE" ATTITUDES

The thoughts
that you think
are up to you,
What you think
is what you do.

Those who are pure in their thinking are happy.
They will be with God.

MATTHEW 5:8

THE "**BE**" ATTITUDES

Increase
the peace.

Those who work to bring peace are happy.
God will call them his sons.

MATTHEW 5:9

THE "**BE**" ATTITUDES

It is good
to do good.

Those who are treated badly for doing good are happy.
The kingdom of heaven belongs to them.

MATTHEW 5:10

Heaven has
a party
when Jesus is born
in a new heart.

There is joy before the
angels of God when one sinner changes his heart.

LUKE 15:10

Into my heart,
Into my heart,
Come into my heart, Lord Jesus.
Come in today,
Come in to stay,
Come into my heart, Lord Jesus.

I stand at the door and knock.
If anyone hears my voice and opens the door,
I will come in and eat with him. And he will eat with me.

REVELATION 3:20

When brother's a bother
and sister's sassy,
pay them with patience.

Love is patient and kind.

1 CORINTHIANS 13:4

God loves the person
who gives happily.

2 CORINTHIANS 9:7

An encouraging word
Deserves to be heard.

Say what people need—
words that will help others become stronger.

EPHESIANS 4:29

When there's nothing to hide, You have peace inside.

If you forgive others for the things they do wrong,
then your Father in heaven will also forgive you
for the things you do wrong.

MATTHEW 6:14

Sing a song and shoo away sorrows.

Come, let's sing for joy to the Lord.
Let's shout praises to the Rock who saves us.

PSALM 95:1

God is faithful.
He is the One who has called you to
share life with his Son,
Jesus Christ our Lord.

1 CORINTHIANS 1:9

A VERSE TO MEMORIZE

Red and yellow,
Black and white,
All are precious
in God's sight.

God accepts anyone
who worships him and does what is right.

ACTS 10:35

Trust and obey — there's no other way!

Trust the Lord with all your heart.

PROVERBS 3:5

Say no when you know
That something is wrong.
Say yes and be blessed
When it's right in God's sight.

Happy is the person who doesn't listen to the wicked. . . .
He doesn't do what bad people do.
He loves the Lord's teachings.
He thinks about those teachings day and night.

PSALM 1:1–2

Manners matter.

Love is not rude.

1 CORINTHIANS 13:5

Worry and frowns Pull the heart down.

Give all your worries to him,
because he cares for you.

1 PETER 5:7

The devil is always evil behind the "d."

Stand against the devil,
and the devil will run away from you.

JAMES 4:7

If you don't know, don't go!

Respect the Lord and refuse to do wrong.

PROVERBS 3:7

The Lord is my shepherd.
I have everything I need.
He gives me rest in green pastures.
He leads me to calm water.
He gives me new strength.

PSALM 23:1–3

All creatures great and small, The Lord God loves them all.

This is how God showed his love to us:
He sent his only Son into the world
to give us life through him.

1 JOHN 4:9

Don't quit or give up,
When struggles you face.
Those who keep trying
will finish the race.

I keep trying to reach the goal and get the prize.

PHILIPPIANS 3:14

God did not give us
a spirit that makes us afraid.
He gave us
a spirit of power
and love and
self-control.

2 TIMOTHY 1:7

A VERSE TO MEMORIZE

Hope is something no one
can ever take away from you.
Only you can send it away.

I pray that the God who gives hope
will fill you with much joy and peace
while you trust in him.

ROMANS 15:13

Love grows,
when love flows.

You must love each other as I have loved you.

JOHN 13:34

God loves you.

The Father has loved us so much!
He loved us so much that we are called children of God.

1 JOHN 3:1

Some books have pictures,
Some make me think,
Some make me laugh,
And some help me cook.

Upstairs, downstairs,
everywhere I look . . .
The Bible is still
The very best book!

Your word is like a lamp for my feet and a light for my way.

PSALM 119:105

Take care of the earth—
For all it's worth!
Don't take this planet for granted.
In all of space, it's the only place
That's fit for the human race.

The Lord God put the man
in the garden of Eden to care for it and work it.

GENESIS 2:15

Let your light shine.

In the same way, you should be a light for other people.
Live so that they will see the good things you do.
Live so that they will praise your Father in heaven.

MATTHEW 5:16

Faith is what you know is true.
Faith is also what you do.

Faith that does nothing is worth nothing.

JAMES 2:20

Give miles of smiles in great big piles.

Happiness makes a person smile.

PROVERBS 15:13

96

Children, obey your parents
the way the Lord wants.
This is the right thing to do.

EPHESIANS 6:1

It's truly amazing
just what they can do —
Those three little words,
"Please" and "Thank you."

Always give thanks to God the Father for everything.

EPHESIANS 5:20

BLESSINGS

1. MOM
2. DAD
3. HOME
4. TEACHER
5. FOOD
6. UNCLE BOB
7. CHURCH
8. FLOWERS
9. THE PARK

Count your many blessings, Name them one by one.

Thanks be to God for his gift that is too wonderful to explain.

2 CORINTHIANS 9:15

Saving cents makes sense.

Wise people store up the best foods and olive oil.

PROVERBS 21:20

Those who go to
God Most High for safety
will be protected
by God All-Powerful.

PSALM 91:1

Helping hands
Make happy hearts.

Serve each other with love.

GALATIANS 5:13

Despise lies.
But be friends
with the truth.

Test everything. Keep what is good.
And stay away from everything that is evil.

1 THESSALONIANS 5:21

Not what you get
But what you give,
Determines the worth
of the life you live.

It is more blessed to give than to receive.

ACTS 20:35

Snowflakes and fingerprints—
You'll always find—
Each one is different, one of a kind.

And just like a snowflake
This, too, is true,
No one else is exactly like you!

I praise you because you made me
in an amazing and wonderful way.

PSALM 139:14

Additional copies of this book and other titles in the
God's Little Instruction Book series
are available at your local bookstore.

God's Little Instruction Book
God's Little Instruction Book II
God's Little Instruction Book—Special Gift Edition
God's Little Instruction Book Daily Calendar
God's Little Instruction Book for Mom
God's Little Instruction Book for Dad
God's Little Instruction Book for Students
God's Little Instruction Book for Graduates

P.O. Box 55388
Tulsa, Oklahoma 74155